Goats Coats and More

Written by
Evelyn Heckhaus

AuthorHouse™ LLC
1663 Liberty Drive
Bloomington, IN 47403
www.authorhouse.com
Phone: 1-800-839-8640

Published by AuthorHouse 10/03/2014

ISBN: 978-1-4969-3591-5 (sc)
978-1-4969-3590-8 (e)

Library of Congress Control Number: 2014915039

Any people depicted in stock imagery provided by Thinkstock are models, and such images are being used for illustrative purposes only. Certain stock imagery © Thinkstock.

This book is printed on acid-free paper.

authorHOUSE®

Goats Coats and More

THE GOAT FAMILY

"We need a bigger house," said Ben's dad. "With our new little boy we need a bigger house and a bigger yard for him and his sister to play in." Ben was just a wee baby in the family when the decision was made to move from the two-bedroom house to a bigger four-bedroom house in a nearby town. A lovely brick house near Ben's grandma was for sale and Ben's family decided to buy it.

Soon a big truck came and stopped out in front of the small house where Ben lived. Beds, chairs, tables, and many assorted boxes were loaded into the truck. The truck headed west on the interstate highway.

Arriving in the next town, the truck stopped at a large brick house next to a fenced in meadow.

"How will we keep our meadow mowed?" asked Ben's mom.

"I'm thinking a family of goats will solve that problem. The goats will have a nice place to nibble and will keep the grass chewed down," said Ben's dad.

Ben took on the chore of feeding the goats on a regular basis. If the goats were not fed, they would bleat loudly and stand near the part of the fence where they were watered and fed.

When Ben's cousins or other young friends came to visit Ben 's family, the goats would get an extra serving of leaves from nearby bushes. It was a great treat for the visitors and the goats to experience the midday snack time.

The first goats were Alpine goats named Phil and Lil, plus a Saanen goat named Snodie. He was one of a kind - a dairy goat from Switzerland. He had short white hair and horns. Later, Joey, Doc, Oreo, Daisy, Scooter, and Buddy were added to the family. The goat family enjoyed keeping the grass in the meadow chewed down.

Ben's dad made a shelter to give the goats shade and protection from stormy weather.

"Look, " said Ben. "Some of the goats are climbing on top of the new shelter! Why do you think they want to do that?"

" I guess the goats prefer climbing to snuggling," said Ben's dad. Occasionally, as they stood on the roof of the shelter, they would stretch their necks to nibble on the leaves of the tree nearby.

"Remember to feed the goats," was heard from Ben's parents every evening after supper. The gray goat Doc was almost always first in line for the evening meal. If he thought the other goats were getting ahead of him, he would nudge them out of the way with his wet nose.

One morning after feeding and watering the goats, Ben called his dad.

"Dad, Daisy did not come up for breakfast. Should we look for her?" asked Ben.

"Sure, I'll help you," said Ben's dad. "Let's look down by the tall trees and then over by the barn." Both of them checked all the corners of the field. Over in the farthest corner of the meadow they found Daisy lying in a clump of grass. Two baby goats were lying next to her.

"Daisy has been busy bringing her babies into the family," said Ben's dad. "She will come up for breakfast when she gets her strength back. Maybe the little ones will be up on their legs by then and can join her." Ben was delighted to be the first to discover the newborn twin goats, which he named Snicker and Doodle. From the coloring of their fur it was determined that Joey and Daisy were their parents.

What fun the goats had frolicking in the meadow. They were a frisky bunch, especially at mealtime. You could see them running from all corners of the meadow, when they saw Ben coming at feeding time.

Once Ben went to feed the goats early in the morning and found one of his goats lying in the grass and not moving. He rushed to find his father to find out if there was a way to revive his goat. Ben 's dad and mom helped to ease the burden of sadness caused by the death of his goat. They explained to Ben that his goat was very old and had fulfilled his purpose in life.

COATS FOR THE GOATS

One winter the temperature dropped very low. Ben's dad was concerned that the goats might not survive the unusual cold weather. He often checked the TV weather station to stay informed of upcoming weather changes.

Seeing that temperatures would fall even lower, Ben's dad bought a blanket. He cut out a paper pattern for a coat for the goats to put their front feet into and would fasten at the front neck under the chin. He took his paper pattern and tried it on one of the goats. It seemed to be a perfect fit.

Next, he placed the pattern on the blanket and realized he could make several coats. Taking some sharp scissors he cut out the coats. There would be a couple of seams to sew closed for a good fit. Using the sewing machine to close the seams, Ben's dad kept breaking the sewing machine needle.

Next, he called Ben's grandma who was a seamstress.

"Why does my machine needle keep breaking?" Ben's dad asked.

" You probably are using the wrong sized needle for your project," said Grandma. "Call your fabric shop and tell the manager which fabric you are working with. You will be told what size needle you need for your project." Ben's dad dashed to the fabric shop and purchased a much larger machine needle. This needle worked just fine.

That evening Ben and his dad went to the meadow and fastened a coat on each goat. All seemed fine. The next morning all goats were still wearing their coats, except one.

"Dad, what do you think Doc did with his coat? I looked around for it, but it was nowhere nearby," said Ben.

After searching all over the meadow, even over by the barn, Ben discovered the missing coat. Doc had chewed his coat fastener, removed his coat, and chewed it into a ragged piece of fabric.

The rigorous activity of biting the coat, tossing it around with his teeth, and chewing it even more had kept Doc busy during the night. The activity must have kept his body temperature at a safe level, because the ice in the water trough was frozen solid.

Ben was really happy that all of his goats, especially Doc, had survived the severe cold temperature during the night.

THE NEW GOAT ON THE BLOCK

One morning Sheriff Jones knocked on the front door. Ben looked out the window and noticed the Sheriffs car in the driveway.

"Ben," he said "we found a young goat wandering down the street a short way from your house. Are you missing one?" Ben went out to the meadow and counted his goats.

"No, sir," Ben said. "All my goats are accounted for."

"Well," said the officer, "could you adopt him for now until we find his owner?"

"Sure," said Ben, "I am certain this new goat will enjoy the company of my goats. Bring him on down and I will introduce him to my goat family."

The little goat had a beautiful coat of black fur. Ben suggested that his family call him "Midnight". Midnight adjusted quickly to his new goat friends and was quite happy nibbling on the grass in the meadow. Midnight learned quickly that when Ben showed up at the fence, it was "eating time". The new goat soon became one of the goat family.

Several months later Sheriff Jones knocked on the front door.

"Ben," he said, "we have found the little goat's proper owner." Ben was saddened to hear the news, because he had grown fond of Midnight. Would this mean that Midnight would return to his owner?

"Do you think Midnight's owner might let me keep him?" asked Ben.

"I'll talk to her for you and let you know her answer," said Officer Jones. He left, but soon returned.

"The lady said you may keep Midnight. She told me the little goat continued to get out of his pen and she cannot take care of him any more," said Sheriff Jones. "He is yours if it is O.K. with your parents".

Ben had a talk with his parents about the added responsibility of a new goat. This would mean he would have to attend to more of his "goat keeping" activities. He would have to promise to add his new responsibilities to his current list of "goat keeping" jobs.

Midnight was adopted by Ben and his family. The little goat was no longer the new goat on the block.

THE MISSING GOATS

"Ben, I need you!" yelled Dad from the door of the red barn hoping Ben could hear him calling.

Strong gusts of wind may have drowned out his voice.

Ben was riding his scooter on the driveway when Dad called. He enjoyed this time in the afternoon. Homework and chores were done and he could spend a few moments on his scooter. He had filled the cat food dishes, checked the litter box, and had even spent time with his younger brother, Nat. He wondered what could be so urgent for Dad to call him to the barn.

Dad called again, "Ben, I need you." The windy day that had the markings of a hurricane had caused the gate to the goat pen to be blown open.

"Dad, what is wrong?" Ben asked as he ran toward the barn. The urgency in Dad's voice troubled Ben.

"I can't find the goats. I believe the strong wind has dislodged the gate and the goats are gone," suggested Dad. "Where they would have gone is the next question."

A gust of wind almost blew Ben off the path to the barn. Signs of an impending downpour were evident. If the goats were not found soon, they could drown in the swollen creek that wound through the nearby woods behind the house.

"Ben, come with me down the path to the house next door. If the goats are going in that direction I will need you to help send them back," said Dad.

Ben and his dad rushed toward the house next door hoping they could find the goats. Pushing through the branches of the trees in the wooded area would be difficult, but Ben and his dad looked there. No goats were there. Ben and his dad headed back to the meadow on the other side of their house.

"I say we check across the street," said Ben. "Those goats can travel fast when they decide they need something to eat. You should see them come running when I take them their grain food in the afternoon."

"Watch out for any trucks or cars as you cross the street," said Dad. Ben headed toward the old school yard across the highway from their house. Checking for oncoming traffic from both directions, he dashed across the street.

"Dad, look over there down the gravel road in front of the old school," shouted Ben. "I think I see a couple of goats. Maybe, the rest of them are nearby." Dad ran ahead of Ben down the gravel road. As he rounded the curve near the old school he could see the rest of the goats enjoying the grass behind the school, unaware of the impending storm.

"Ben, see if you can get behind the goats to help me chase them home," called Dad from the end of the gravel road. Reaching the grassy area Ben could help nudge them towards home. Having the goats cross the highway safely would be a challenge.

Ben picked up two sticks he found beneath a nearby tree. He hoped that the noise from rapping the sticks would motivate the goats to head toward home. Dad saw Ben's strategy. He began clapping his hands while Ben rapped the sticks. The goats obligingly headed down the gravel road back toward the house. As they reached the road, the goats paused. They seemed to realize their safety would be compromised if they dashed across. Dad's clapping and Ben's rapping stopped long enough to wait for a break in the traffic.

"O.K. goats, head for home. The storm will soon be here and you will be in the middle of a hurricane," shouted Ben's dad. The hand clapping and stick rapping encouraged the goats to start across the road.

"Getting ten goats to go in the same direction at one time might be a challenge," said Ben "but here we go." The goats haltingly stepped onto the road.

"If they can get across before any more trucks or cars come," thought Ben, "everything will be fine." A drizzle of rain began as the goats bumped each other trying to get across the road. The slick road caused a couple of the goats to slide sprawling in the middle of the road.

"Come on goats," chided Ben. "We are almost home. Now go!" Ben gently touched the rumps of the two fallen goats, which caused them to jump up and head home.

"Dad, I think we can get them in the pen before the storm hits. Clap some more," said Ben. Dad responded and the goats moved as Ben had anticipated. Down the driveway beside the house and toward the red barn they scampered. As Ben held the goat pen gate wide open, his dad directed the goats back inside. Ben slammed the gate shut.

"It's closed good this time," shouted Ben, "and not a moment too soon 'cause here comes the rain." A loud clap of thunder rolled across the heavens and the rain began to beat down on their heads.

What a great story Ben would have to tell his mom and his sister of the adventures with the missing goats.

MYSTERY AT THE SHELTER

Ben's nanny goats had added a few new baby goats during the fall. Now there were plenty of goats to nibble the grass in the meadow. It was Ben's dad's idea that goats would keep the grass in the meadow under control by chomping the grass short.

"Dad", said Ben, "I think we need another shelter for our goats. Now that we have more goats, one shelter doesn't have enough room for all of them to get out of the rain."

"Well", said Ben's dad, "this weekend I will get us some wood. You can help me build something." Saturday arrived. They took the measuring tape out to the original shelter. They checked the height, length and width of the building. Ben and his dad decided to just attach an addition to the current shelter. They headed to town to locate some planks for the shelter. They also bought some nails. Ben knew his dad had a saw and hammer to complete the job. On the way back from shopping for wood, Ben asked his dad,

"Dad, are we making the shelter exactly like the first one we made?"

"Yep", said his dad, "that's why we did all the measuring. You get to "saw" the planks in half for the shelter side while I am putting down the anchor boards to give the shape and size."

"0. K. Dad," said Ben, "you let me do this once before, so I know what to do this time."

Ben's dad laid out the boards for the Ben to "saw" in half. This would be the side of the new addition. He next laid out the boards for the back of the shelter. He had saved some tin from making the first shelter. The piece of tin would cover the whole roof. By supper time the shelter was finished. Ben and his dad were a good team.

Ben watched on the rainy days to see which goats were smart enough to protect them selves from the storm. A few goats used the old shelter and some used the new shelter. Only two goats stood outside the shelter in the rain.

"Why would those two goats stand out in the rain?" Ben asked.

"That is just a mystery," said Ben's dad. Several weeks went by. Cold winter days were forecasted by the TV weatherman. Ben was concerned about his goats being warm enough on the unusually cold days.

"Dad," said Ben, "you know those lamps we took with us on our camping trip to keep us warm?"

"Yes," said Ben's dad, "what are you thinking?"

"Could we hang one in each shelter to make it a little warmer?" said Ben. "We could pound a long nail on one of the walls to hang a lamp. That ought to keep us from losing any goats due to the extreme cold."

"I will take care of that after supper," said Ben's dad. "I will go out after supper and pound in a couple of nails to hang the lamps. Then I'll get some fuel for our lamps. Let's just hope our goats will appreciate all our efforts to keep them from freezing in this cold weather." Ben's dad carried out his promise after they had enjoyed Ben's favorite supper—pizza and pineapple salad.

The temperature dropped below freezing that same night. Ben worried about his goats and how they would adjust to the heat lamps. He even dreamed about his goats huddling around the heat lamps. Ben had a fireplace in his house where he could warm up nearby. His couch had a crocheted afghan he could snuggle under.

The next morning Ben anxiously jumped in his clothes and headed out to the goat pasture. He was quite surprised to see that except for one goat all the other goats huddled in the old shelter near the heat lamp. Only one goat was in the new shelter near the heat lamp. Ben wondered what could have made all the goats (except the one) snuggle together in the old shelter. Many questions passed through his mind. Did the one goat smell so bad that his fellow goats did not want to share the heat lamp with him? Did the one goat chase the rest away like a bully? Did the new shelter still smell like a new shelter? What would make all the rest of the goats cuddle in the old shelter and exclude the one goat?

When Ben shared his thoughts with his dad, Ben's dad said, "We may never know the answer to why the goats excluded the one goat. This will forever remain a mystery to us. This will just have to be the unsolved mystery of the cold night at the shelter."

Printed in the United States
By Bookmasters